The Quindecim Anthology

Sunday Hart

Presentation by *BookLeaf Publishing*

Web: www.bookleafpub.com

E-mail: info@bookleafpub.com

ISBN: 9789357212878

First edition 2023

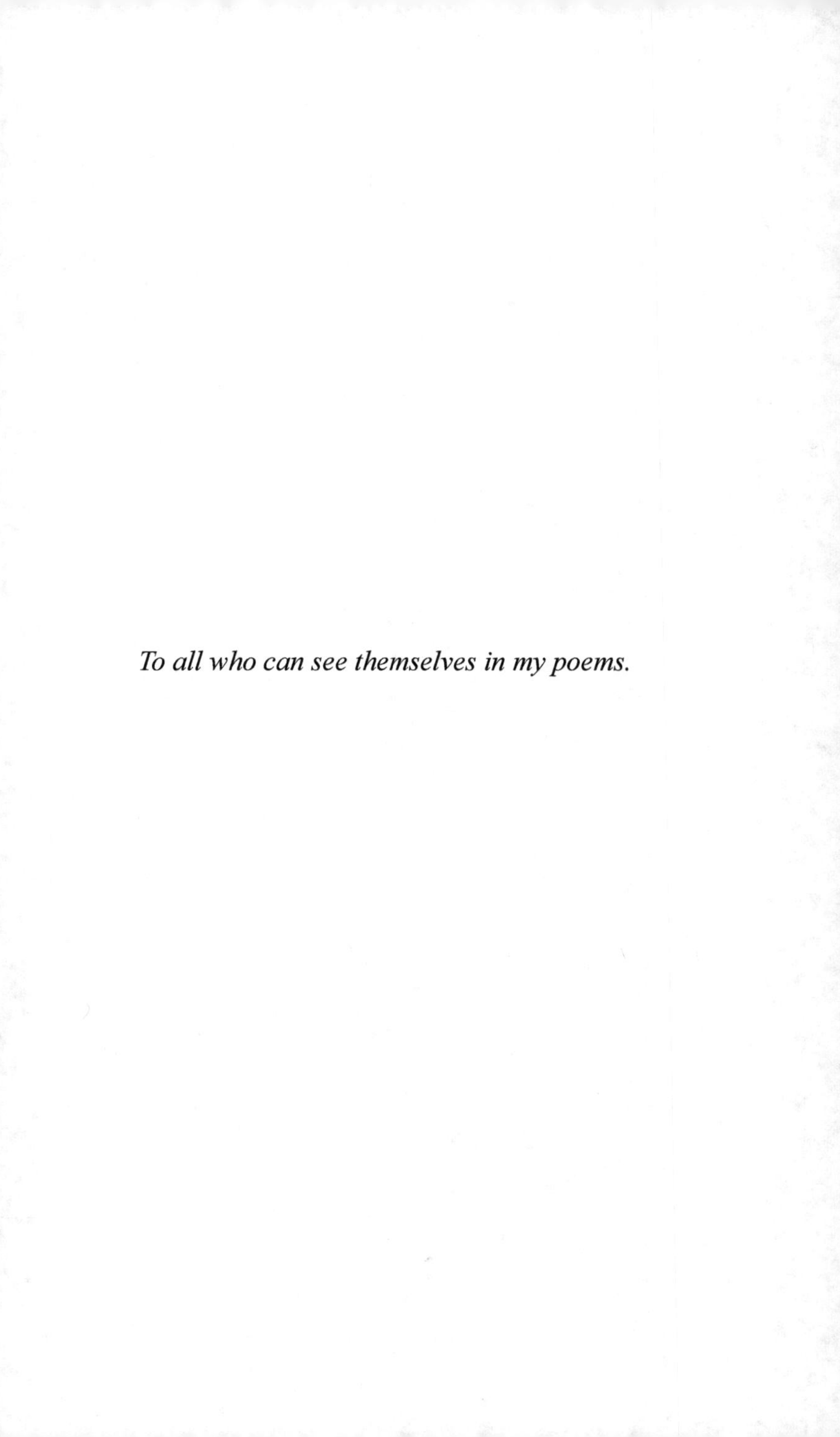

To all who can see themselves in my poems.

PREFACE

This book is a collection of poems written throughout my life.
I ask that you read it with grace and an open mind.

Some poems are better written than others, I could have adjusted and rewritten some of them during this process, but it is my belief that we are worthy in all our forms of growth and development and I wanted to honour my younger self by staying true to them.

.

Senses coming in to focus

Eyes still closed

I can feel the warmth
And hear the breath

I can feel the caress

Is this a rebirth

·

Serene and content, their anger they vent

To close my eyes
It's me they despise

No more to give
They're insistent I live

Understanding strangers
All viewed as extreme dangers

Miserable and alone
It's this place they call home

•

You'll understand when you have your own
You'll understand when you are grown

And unfortunately you are right
I now truly understand the plight

I would/could never treat a child that way
And I can't believe you ever thought that okay

When I was younger I thought 'it can't be that
bad'
But now I am grown I see you were mad

I do understand now that I am grown
And what I get is that I never had a home

I will never apologise for being who I am
I will never apologise for going to poetry slams
I will never apologise for being "cringe" as you
say
I will never apologise for going out to play

You call me child, like that's a bad thing

I feel sorry for you, you never let your soul sing

Next time do it properly
You grit your teeth and said
So this time to you
I really am dead

Laundry

I want to tear off my skin and sinew
And scratch my bones

I want to scrape away at them until they
resemble toothpicks

Then I can wring out my muscles like a dirty
dish rag,
And drape the over my new skeleton

I can stretch out my sinews 'til they're raggedy
and limp,
Then thread them throughout my body

I step back into my skin and pull it on like a big
winter coat

I tug it into place,
It doesn't fit quite like before,
But I no longer feel like I'm suffocating

I feel lighter and brighter

For now.

Where noon is night, and night is noon
Where the sea is black and the sky is blue
Where fire is water and light is dark
Where all the cats resolve to bark
Where hot is cold and bitter is sweet
Where Romeo and Juliet never meet
Where screams are whispers and love is hate
Where no one really believes in fate
Where lies are truth and flowers bite
Where lovers always tend to fight
Where sadness is consuming and happiness
never comes
Where you have no fingers and only thumbs
Where tears are endless and pain is the norm
Where everyday a child is born
Where no one dares to breathe a breath, just in
case it signals death
Where lies run deep and promises shallow
Where the cheeriest sight is the gallows
Where thunder is lightning and doors are bricked
up
Where I always end up getting cut
Where hearts are broken every day
Where no one knows what to say
Where anything solid is actually sheer
Where I say welcome, welcome to here.

To step into a world
That is twisted and curled
Is sometimes all that you need
It can make your heart lift, swell and bleed
Your thoughts bury deep
And cause you to lose your sleep
It can give you friends to spare
But in the end they're all shared
You feel so alone and empty inside
You've laughed, been angry and cried
But the end result is an entirely different view
Of the new world, that's now inside of you

.

I am not like the others
I don't have many lovers
Touch me I shudder
Much to the disappointment of my mother

Many dream of making sweet love
But me? None of the above

A kiss makes me wretch
As if it's sucking my life like a letch

A hug is bareable
But a smile is uncompareable

A secret look, shared between two
That's all I want from my beau

Wash day

Seven hours in the chair
Three hours mum pulling at my hair

2 smacks with the comb for my tender head
I daren't move while I'm lying in bed

Hands reaching to touch and pull the braids
I duck and I weave and I throw all the shade

My crown, my heritage, my love and my joy
We feel it all, whether girl, enby or boy

.

Screaming, crying, shaking in the street
And you all walk by, not missing a beat

'How can they be so callous, uncaring?' I
thought
Look at me standing here, clearly distraught

I raise hand to my mouth and suddenly realise
The screaming, crying, shaking is happening
inside.

You show your concern
And my eyes begin to burn
All these voices in my head
All those tears silently shed
I try and tell of my pain
But it's all in vain
I don't want to hurt you
Telling you of the blood I drew
You try and comfort me
But all I want to do is flee
Run far away from you
So I don't make you blue

Multiple things can be true
I can love them and be into you

I can be happy and also sad
About the life I never had

People think it's all so easy
Like life is cheerful, chill and breezy

But you see, it's just not true
Because I can still love them, and be into you

Please stop hurting me, I've had enough now
Please stop torturing me, I beg with furrowed
brow
Please stop berating me, I have nothing left to
live for
Please stop tearing me apart.   I try and run
for the door
Please stop this relentless assault, I don't know
what I did!
You turn to me and with twisted smile sneer 'All
you did was live'

.

Doctors notes:

Patient is Caucasian.   Wrong, I'm passing.
Patient is clean, presentable, well put together.
Presentable, sure; but I haven't showered or
brushed my teeth in three weeks, at least.
Patient seems disinterested.   I'm here against
my will.
Patient has no history of sexual assault.   That
one's on me. I lied.

Stomach twisting, turning and jumping
My little heart is rapidly thumping
I don't know how, or why, or when
But somewhere I've lost my peace and zen
I feel ever so sick and ever so tired
This must be anything other than inspired
I despise these feelings
So I avoid such dealings
But somewhere along the line, it has become fun
Even if all I want to do is turn and run

.

Just let me swim in my river of red

Without me getting tied to a bed

Let me cut open my present with complete
fearless glee

Just let me, just let me, just let me be free

Like a child losing grip on their favourite
balloon

I stretch and I reach but it's gone far too soon

But I never give up hope, and for that it has to be
said,

That maybe I should be tied to a bed

Death is not something I fear
In fact it is something I hold most dear

However when it comes for those I love
(A maximum of three, nothing above)

Death becomes a most fearsome beast
And I fear that those three will be it's next feast

At dusk I wake from nightmare after nightmare
It's becoming too heavy for my soul to bear

．

She flows and floats; delicate and light

But I'm sure if she wanted she could bring
endless night

She could bellow and stomp and be altogether
foul

She could rip and tear and give endless howl

.

There're two people inside of my head
It's like my skin is being constantly shed

I don't know which one is about to come out
It could be the one that hits, screams and shouts

One keeps ruining the life of the other
It's as if they like to see them suffer

Chunks of consciousness missing from both
Constantly spinning out, uncontrollable growth

I wish they could understand all I want is peace
Even if that means one stays on a leash

The child never had

They called you selfish, they called you silly,
they said you didn't know what you meant.

I am grateful to be the falling domino. Give me a
minute, just let me vent.

I am glad to have been spared the neglect and
abuse you'd have lay on me, through no fault of
your own.

We share the same thought, that it is ludicrous to
have a child when one is so ill, I'd have ended up
your clone.

It is insanity to ignore reality and think a child
will 'fix' you. It honestly feels like they just don't
have a clue.

We both know that you can't be fixed, so we do
damage control instead.
And we did it. I'm glad we could do this
together, thank you for sparing me the dread.